Made in United States
Orlando, FL
09 April 2022

16668111R00061